HELP!

Is this love

HELP!

Is this love?

Joseph Mvula

Joseph Mvula

Edited and proof read by Prisca Mwanza and Florence Joy Mkandawire

Layout: Mwamba Brian

Printed & bound in Zambia by:
Litovia Limited
+260 977 452 739

ISBN: 978-9982-70-050-4

p. : 136

Dedication

I dedicate this book to two of very important girls in my life. To my wife, Naomi Chabala Mvula whom I have come to love and appreciate since we met at a youth group church meeting. My love Naomi, together we have grown to love, respect, treasure and cherish each other. I can't imagine what kind of life I could have been living had I not met you. I could have been single, lonely and sad but you have brought a great sense of joy to my heart and fulfillment beyond explanation. You are the best and everything I learnt about love from you is in this book.

To my daughter Adara Walusungu Mvula, your birth brought so much joy to our hearts and this book is dedicated to you that as you grow up you will make informed decisions when it comes to matters of love.

Acknowledgement

To God almighty, the source of my livelihood, the savior of my soul; I give thanks.

To my dear mother, a woman who sacrificed so much to see me grow and become a great man, I give thanks.

To my dear spiritual father Bishop Joe Imakando, a man that preached me into my destiny and trusted me with being part of the shepherds in the sheepfold of Bread of life church, I give thanks.

To my dear friend and true brother Pastor Gideon K. Chibwe, a man that believes in my dreams and puts up with my weaknesses, always there to encourage me when I am discouraged, I give thanks.

To the pastoral team at Bread of Life Church International; Reverend Shadrick Chisulo, pastors George Msendo, Luther Maseko, Jatto Phiri, Oscar Mumba, Joseph Chilumbu, Crispin Suya, Elias Mwalusaka and all those not mentioned, your love and support is highly appreciated.

All my friends and family, I am very grateful for your support.

May the Lord richly bless you!

Table of Contents

INTRODUCTION

You are holding in your hands a book that can change the love story of your life for good. Deep thoughtfulness and sincere dedication has been given in the process of writing this book. I know for in no doubt that many other books carrying a similar message have been written and different views given over this subject matter, LOVE; and I should from the bottom of my heart mention that we may not be in total agreement over some issues regarding this subject with other writers but I do know that we may all provide some helpful information that can add value to the love stories of millions of people worldwide. In the pages of the book of your love story features this book and I hope and pray that it will be a chapter that will be exciting and informative.

Bishop T.D Jakes in his book "Before you do" made an interesting observation when he wrote:

"A single person who longs for a heart's companion is like the woman described in the Bible who had ten coins and lost one. "Does she not light a lamp, sweep the house and search carefully until she finds it?" Luke 15:8 NIV

You may have all the nine coins dearly and cleverly in your possession. You have the title, the job, the education, the home, the car the clothes. You are at the top of the game professionally but personally you do not have the coin for which you so desperately long. In such a situation, it's tempting to think, "I have these areas going for me, why get hung up on a man? I have my nine coins, why look for a tenth?" it's because you know in your heart that the tenth makes the set complete. In other words it is tempting to try and compensate for what you don't have but long for.

I recommend that you be honest with yourself and don't try to pretend that you haven't lost a coin when you sense something is missing."

These words represent many people that are pretending that the "nine coins" are all they need but the one coin that would make the set complete is missing.

I don't know what your interest is in reading this book but, one thing that I know for sure, is that every human being is in need of love. Humans are affectionate beings. God made you and me, with an inner yearning to be accepted and appreciated- to love and be loved.

I must mention on the onset that the principle in this book is; never do experiments with your heart. Simply put, do not involve yourself in an intimate relationship until you are sure of what you are doing and are ready to do it with an understanding of the consequences that may follow thereafter.

The absence of love in someone's life can be a source of immense frustration and pain. You can have everything you need physically but it is only when your emotional needs are met that you will have a sense of belonging and fulfillment. People across the globe do a lot of things to find true love. Many people, out of deep rooted frustrations and a strapped self-perceptions, have grown hostile toward the great need and value of love because, they have tried hard to make it work and it has not worked and as a result, they speak ill of the very thing that would bring them great cheer and calm of heart. They discredit the feeling of love. Because their past attempts to find true love landed them into serious emotional problems, they have concluded that all people are the same- liars and cheaters but little do they know that by concluding all people are the same, they include themselves among the said cheaters and liars.

As a life coach, preacher and teacher of God's word, I have met many people desperately in need of love. Anxious to fall in love, they are so distressed, panic-stricken, and troubled about the absence of someone to love them and you could actually be one of them. Almost on a daily basis, I have come across people that are so affected by the absence of love. A young lady confided in one of my colleagues in the pastoral office and tearfully told him that she had everything but all she needed was a man to marry her. She had a good paying job, a car, a house and all the material things she needed but the absence of a man was a great source of loneliness and dissatisfaction in her life. Loneliness, that deep sited feeling of being alone even in the company of people can drive one insane. That is why I can confidently say to you that whoever you are and whatever position of authority you hold in society, you need love. Yes love is the only legitimate means through which loneliness can be done away with. Everything else will only expose the hidden wound caused by the absence of love more and more. Many people have tried to fill up the emptiness caused by the absence of love by buying a new car, finding a new job, moving around the world, taking time off from routine work for leisure and pleasure but all this and many other efforts have been despised by the compelling power of the need and desire to love and be loved. There can never be a substitute to love. Love is the greatest need of the human race and God knows it. Of all the great things God Almighty could have done for mankind, He decided to love us. God loved man with all the faults and imperfections that characterized him. He loves us. Love is the greatest need of mankind. Mankind can never be loved enough and that is why God loves us eternally. The only proof that mankind is human is his ability to love. It is not human to fail to love.

The title of this book gives you what it is all about. It has been written for the sole purpose of helping anyone who is considering sharing his or her life with another person, to understand and learn some guiding principles that can help him or her to succeed in attaining the goal of finding true love. Most of the principles in this book are from my own life experiences as far as matters of love are concerned and some are from a wealthy pool of testimonies of many people I have met who have had good and bad experiences as they attempted to find someone to love and would love them back. I also carried out a research on this great human need and I gathered some lessons that could change your love life for good.

As we enter into this great adventure of exploring some principles that can lead us into some insights to understanding the greatest need of all; love, I encourage you to read patiently and evaluate yourself against the principles shared in this book. Read carefully because patience is one key factor that you need to get the best out of this great piece of writing and then use some of these principles to get you on track on your quest to find true love.

Enjoy the adventure and let us meet in love world. Otherwise, I am already here and it is great. Anxiously waiting for you!

Prayer point

- pray that God will give you the grace to understand what you will read in this book
- pray for emotional wholeness and healing in your life
- pray that this book will not be a sheer waste of precious time
- pray that your life will not be in a mess

Amen

CHAPTER ONE

READINESS FOR A RELATIONSHIP

How do I know I am ready for a relationship? Many people have asked this question many times. They want to know when they are ready to enter into a relationship commitment. I must say that a relationship is not something that one should get into carelessly or thoughtlessly because other than the good feelings of falling in love, a relationship will positively or negatively affect your whole life. A relationship if not prepared for can adversely affect your whole life. Many people have opted to end their lives because they could not cope with the pressures and pains that come with entangling in a love relationship without proper preparation. There are consequences for not being ready for the actions we take. You must be ready before getting in a relationship. The trouble however is in determining ones readiness for a life time relationship commitment. Often I am asked, what age do you recommend for a relationship? This is a difficult question to answer because; age does not always mean one is prepared for a relationship. I have seen young adults still squatting at their parents' homes doing absolutely nothing; just eating their food and I have also seen younger people who have become independent and are responsible over things that a young adult should be responsible for. The issue then is not how old a person is but it is in how responsible and mature a person is to accommodate the challenges and responsibilities of interpersonal relationships. In this context, I mean a love relationship. There are many factors that can help in determining how ready an individual is for a relationship but the basic one is that of being responsible enough to handle a relationship.

Below are seven things to consider when determining your readiness to get into a relationship.

1. *Are you ready to be accountable?*
   This is one of the vital ways of assessing if you are ready for a relationship. If you want to start some secret love affair that only you and your partner know about, you are not ready for a relationship. This does not mean you should go about advertising your relationship to everyone you meet but there must be some kind of openness

and accountability when starting up a relationship. If you are a lady and a man proposes to you, ask him if he is ready to make the relationship accountable e.g. to your pastor or someone you very much respect. If he shows signs of uneasiness and gives you excuses, do not accept his proposal. He is after something else other than your heart. You don't have to imagine what that is because what you will imagine is what he really wants from you- your attractive body! Men use what is outside but they marry what is inside. If there is nothing to marry inside, they will use what they see outside and leave you. A man is only willing to wait for what is inside. For what is outside, he can't wait.

When you are truly ready for a relationship, you will have nothing to hide. Let me tell you the truth, if you cannot tell your parents or pastor about your relationship, you are not ready. Why is your relationship a secret? Ask yourself. What are you hiding that you don't want people to know? I have come to conclude that we often hide things when we know deep down our hearts that there is something wrong with them. In fact a relationship is good news and I have never seen any one that was not keen to share good news with others. It is actually not in us humans to hide good things. Humans like to show off. By the way many relationships that start secretly are usually full of compromises such as fornication.

2. *Would you be free and happy to introduce your partner to your ex or someone you had a crash on if need be?*

    This does not mean that you should look for your ex (i.e. someone you were in a relationship with and are no longer together) to prove that you have moved on. No, it simply means that in the event you meet him/her would you be free and happy to introduce the new man/lady.

    You say "No!" well, you are not ready. If you truly and honestly love the person you are with right now, you will not have mixed feelings as to whether you should introduce him/her to your ex or someone you used to admire. Failure to introduce your partner for unclear reasons imply that you still have hopes of getting things fixed with your former partner and thus introducing the new one may kill your hopes and aspirations.

You cannot be in a relationship and still maintain hopes of getting back with someone you once dated or had a crush on. You are not ready.

I once got in a relationship were my partner said she would only be sure of us after one year and there was no guarantee that after the set period things would turn to my favor. She even refused to introduce me to her siblings and told me she would only do so after that one year test. Oh I ran for my dear heart! I indefinitely ended the relationship because I did not have time to waste.

You should also realize that you will always meet people who will appear to be better than your partner in intellect, physical appearance, financially and in many other areas of life. But true love that is born from a mature heart appreciates people for who they are. Your partner may not be the only "fish" in the sea but he/she is the only type of that fish in the river. If someone else caught that fish before you, I assure you, that could have been the only type of that fish in the river and you could never find another of that kind.

So are you ready to introduce him or her or are you still hoping the other person will miraculously come back into your life? If you have such hopes, sorry, you are not ready.

3. *Will you be proud and satisfied with that relationship?*
    Will you be comparing your relationship with others'? It is okay to be inspired by another relationship that is making progress in achieving its objective of marriage. Yes, I said it right. The major objective of any relationship should be marriage. Anything else is a sheer waste of time.

    Many will argue and say that before you commit yourself you must experiment to see whether he or she is the one or not but my humble recommendation is not to enter into a relationship at all when you are not sure.

    Many young people are wasting their precious time in relationships that are going nowhere. Instead of spending that time developing their lives, they waste it seeing movies with someone who will never marry them. I will later discuss this whole issue of valuing your time as you consider making a commitment to a relationship.

If other peoples relationships make you feel embarrassed and insecure about your own, then you are not ready to be in a relationship.

Remember the famous saying, "One bird in your hand is better than a thousand in the bush." Yes, it is very tempting to want to take off for the bush soothing an idea that it will be so easy to catch one or even more birds that are flying over your head and so you decide to thoughtlessly throw away that one and only bird that you have nourished for a good and long period of time. But no sooner do you realize that it is not that easy to catch another bird than you start the search in the bush and if you do manage to catch one, it just dawns on you that you will have to start feeding this new bird because it wasn't taken care of so well by its first owner or owners. It is so malnourished. At this point you realize that what you had in your hands at first was better. Regrettably you look around hoping the bird you carelessly let go could pass by only to see it in the hands of another hunter better skilled than you. You cry and cry but all the crying are wasted tears because the new hunter is not willing to give you back the old bird. While you are trying to wipe the tears off your face as you accept that the old bird is gone and someone else owns it, the new bird in protest to your visible desire to get back your old bird flies off your hands and there you remain without a bird in your hands. There, you tearfully look around wishing you could even find a dead bird but all of them are gone, taken by hunters that are serious with owning birds.

I hope you get the point. It is loud and clear. You must be satisfied and content with what you have because what you do not have is not yours.

4. *Are you willing to invest your time into that relationship?*
A relationship is a responsibility that demands your attention almost on a daily basis. In the book "keeping your covenant" from the home builder series, it is noted that, "a relationship is a living thing- it thrives with attention and withers when ignored" Think twice before you jump into a relationship or even before you continue in one

because it will require your attention. Someone said, "Time is money." So are you ready to invest it in your relationship. Are you too occupied to give quantity and quality time to your partner? If not, you are not ready for a relationship. Quantity means giving enough and satisfying time to your partner. Quality means giving the best of yourself to your partner. You can't just be staring at your partner like a zombie, add something positive to your partner's wellbeing. Let me also advice the ladies, never to move into the houses of their boyfriends to cohabit. A woman that willingly moves into the boy friend's house to live with him and even sharing intimacy with him unconsciously sends a message to the man that she is cheap and he should never take her seriously. He will use you and most likely he will walk away from you after having sex with you. Then you will be heartbroken and you will cry.

A Research on cohabiting was taken by Linda Waite a professor of psychology (June 1999, University of Chicago) and this below is an excerpt of the summary of part of her findings.

"......Couples with no intention of marrying who decide to cohabit are forming unstable living arrangements that can have negative effects on their emotional, financial and sometimes physical well-being.

Waite also found that these social arrangements may cause serious problems for children raised in households headed by cohabiting couples.

Waite, an expert on family life, studied census reports, the National Survey of Families and Households, the National Health and Social Life Survey and other data to appraise the costs and benefits of cohabitation. She found that men and women who cohabit are more likely than married people to experience partner abuse and infidelity and less likely to receive assistance from family members than married couples.....".

My advice is that never enter into a relationship when you are not ready to marry and never live with a person who is not your spouse. You will save yourself a lot of untold miseries, pains, losses, frustrations and many other negatives consequences for doing so.

5. Are you able to use your time wisely?

In as much as it is very vital to invest time in a relationship, it is also very important to examine how much of that time you are spending or ready to spend in a relationship. If a relationship is going to consume all your time, you are not ready for that relationship. If a relationship is going to demand for all of your energies, it is not adding anything of value to your life. Remember, you are an individual relating or intending to relate with another individual, so a relationship should not infringe you of the blessing of individuality. You have a personal life to live apart from the attachment to other people. If you cannot use your time wisely in a relationship, you are not ready for it.

6. Are you ready to invest your money in a relationship?

Can you invest in your relationship financially? Remember, a relationship is a responsibility. If you are greedy with your money, if you cannot support your partner financially when need arises, if you are a person who just wants to receive financial support from your partner but are not willing to reciprocate, you are not ready for a relationship. Selfishness is reflected by one's unwillingness to help another in need. If you are selfish, you cannot be in a happy and fulfilling relationship. Some ladies have this wrong notion of wanting to always receive from their men but that is not right. As a lady, you can give money to your man as well. Take him out for a good treat, and let him know that you are not after his pocket but you love him for being a good and loving man. Yes, a man has the primary responsibility to provide financially in a relationship because he is the man but a lady must not take it for granted, and just sit by waiting for the man to do everything monetary in a relationship. If you are such a lady that milks poor guys, may God deliver you from the spirit of greed! I mean that is so unfair of you. You are being selfish. Come on; don't give me that indifferent attitude. Show your man what you are made of, a good heart. Stingy, that's not like you.

7. Are you ready to protect your partner?

At times the integrity of your partner will be at stake. Okay, let's face it; people we love can sometimes do weird things like kissing your pet!

You may hear rumors, disparaging ones about your partner. But rumors should be treated as rumors unless proven otherwise. I remember being told by a well-meaning classmate in high school that she saw my 'girlfriend' walking hand in hand with some funny guy. Oh I fumed! My heart beat faster. I couldn't even eat. But guess what, it was just a rumor. I did some investigations, and learned it wasn't her.

Are you ready to defend your partner? If you are one who easily believes negative unsubstantiated reports, you are not ready for a relationship. You may hear embarrassing and character assassinating rumors that spread like wild fire and your partner will need you to standby and support him/her, especially if they are falsely accused but if you cannot support him or her in such times, you are not ready for a relationship.

Examine yourself against the points above and see if you are ready for a relationship.

Prayer points

- Pray that God will help you to ascertain how ready you are for a relationship

- Pray that you shall not waste your precious time dating someone when you are not ready for a relationship

- Pray that God will help you not to waste your time through getting in a relationship that is going no where

Amen

CHAPTER TWO

SEVEN SYMPTOMS OF INFATUATION

Now hold it right there, you could be 'head over hills' about some individual whom most likely you will never meet and if you did, prospects of you getting in a relationship with them are very slim, close to zero if not impossible and you know it but you just cannot help but love them. You are in love! At least that is what you feel- love. Well the bitter truth is that you could be infatuated. Infatuation is a state of being completely carried away by unreasonable passion or feelings of love. There is usually an obsession and an object of desire that may or not be attainable.

An example of infatuation is wishing your neighbors' wife can die so you can assume the role of wife to the husband when she is buried. You are mad! Of course you think this is unreasonable. "How can one wish her neighbor dead to take over the role of wife?" You are wondering. You are right to think that is wacky and it is. Things that people do when infatuated rightly put, are wacky. Example, engaging in a relationship with a married person is total and pure madness but many people do that. They never care about the devastating effects it would have on the family of this foolish man or woman that goes out of his or her matrimonial home to start an affair. Upon being found out, it may lead to a divorce that can deprive children of parental care and love. In short what I am saying is that if you cannot use common sense to weigh the feasibility of a possible relationship with someone, whether it can work or not, you are infatuated. Remember that the prime goal of a relationship is marriage. This essentially, rules out the possibility of having a fruitful and meaningful relationship with a person that is already married.

Now, I am sure in one way or another, you have had your share of this time wasting animal called infatuation. Remember those pictures of some celebrity that you downloaded online or maybe excerpts of photos from magazines, and you fantasized about how sweet it would be to date them? Oh shame, it wouldn't and will never happen. You are wasting precious but misguided emotions. You can as well forget about that person because it will never work. Find something to do instead of wasting your emotional energy on something that will never yield any results.

Below are symptoms of infatuation:

1. Impatience

An inability to wait is a symptom of infatuation. If you just want him/her under whatever circumstances then you are infatuated. Men get easily infatuated because they get attracted to women by what they see so if you are a lady and this man seems to be madly in love with you, do not be deceived, he is likely infatuated by your good looks. If you can't take time to build a long lasting relationship, if you cannot wait to jump into a relationship until you are sure of your decision, you are infatuated. They say, "True love waits." So if you are really in love with that person, why can't you wait for a while until you know and be sure they are the one? There is no such a thing as love at first sight. Love is something people grow into. It may start with mere interactions on a common interest such as a subject in a particular course in college and several other interests and with time they develop romantic feelings for each other and eventually may fall in love. In true love there are always common interests. If you feel you are in love with someone but cannot flow together on common interests, it is not love. The Bible says God created Eve for Adam as a suitable helper. How could she be a suitable helper if she did not have common interests with him? I am sure Adam and Eve could watch football together without fighting over the remote control!

2. Selfishness

Just wanting things to go your way; caring less about the needs and desires of the other person; wanting to be understood and not willing to understand; wanting to get but withholding much; getting emotionally offended when your partner disagrees with you are all signs of infatuation. You are too selfish to be trusted with a heart. Yes I said it. You are so selfish.

I heard a story of a man who dreaded giving but delighted in receiving. One day he fell into a swimming pool but didn't know how to swim. A passer-by ran to the pool and started shouting

"GIVE me your hand!" the man drowning could not stretch out his hand but continued getting weaker and weaker sinking. The passer-by thought twice and shouted, "Please TAKE my hand!" hearing this, the drowning man summoned strength and stretched out his hand to take the hand of his rescuer.

The man was going to die because of his selfishness. He could not give his hand out but he was willing to take the hand of another. In his thoughts, giving out his hand was synonymous with losing out.

In a true and loving relationship, mutual sharing is a traditional practice. Looking out for the best interest of the person you love should not be a burden but a delight. If you always feel you are losing whenever you do something for your partner or the person you are interested in, you are not in true love.

3. Sudden Withdrawal

Infatuation treats the person whom you are infatuated over as a faultless and perfect person but soon the real person appears and you tend to withdraw from him or her. You wonder what happened to you to fall for them. I mean when you look at the nose now! Holy heavens! I have laughed at myself over some girls I fell for in the past. What on earth was that?!

All that attracted you to the person is neutralized and you feel no fascination or connection to that person. Have you ever felt so drawn to someone and suddenly you realize you were not thinking straight? I mean at that time, nothing mattered but the person you so wished to have to yourself and yourself alone. But now when you come to think of it, you are shocked you wasted your emotions. You were, or are still infatuated. A relationship that is birthed from the womb of infatuation never lasts. It usually has a hurtful end.

4. **Sexual Demands**

In this sexually active age, sex is viewed as part of the fun of dating and many people would not stay in a relationship where sex is not present. For them, love is synonymous with sex but we have already learnt that true love will wait. Ladies here is a tip, if you use your body to attract attention from men that is all they will come for; your body.

Infatuation never respects the will of another person. In fact, a strong desire to have sex with the person whom you have just met is one of the major symptoms of infatuation. It comes from a strange attraction to the outward appearance of the person. In fact, infatuation is one of the signs that you could be under the control of the spirit of lust. That sounds superstitious right? But to tell you the truth, there is always a spiritual influence on people that have strange sexual urges.

When infatuated, you may have this urge to have sex with the person and you will get very emotionally hurt if the person says no. infatuation says no sex no fun. It is boring.

5. Abnormal Jealousy
Jealousy is acceptable to a certain extent in a relationship but if your jealousy is uncontrollable,

you are infatuated. If you can't just stand seeing an opposite sex talking to your partner, if you will always want to find out what they are talking about and why, you are infatuated. For heaven's sake and before your face turns blue they are talking about bananas!

Look, when you met that person, you did not meet them on Mars but on Earth and they had friends and family, so you can't come to break their friendships with other people. Unless out of concern of some destructive flaws in the people your partner calls friends, you can advise accordingly but other than that, you should give your partner freedom to socialize. I mean socializing not flirting. After all you are not always where your partner is. If he or she means to cheat they can do it.

6. **Suspicion**

If you are finding yourself suspicious of your partner's ways all the time, you are under infatuation. True love trusts. If you cannot trust your partner and you are ever suspicious of them cheating on you or about to end the relationship for some unknown reasons, you are infatuated. Why should you spend time imagining the waste of your partner and in the first place why continue with someone you can't trust?

7. Easily Taking Offense

If you easily get offended by some things your partner does, you are infatuated. The true and perfect person you are trying to date does not exist. True love does not easily take offense but if you think you are always right, and never wrong, you are infatuated. In true love, you will always take responsibility of your wrongs and will seek to make peace. Why do you easily get upset? It likely means you are not in love.

Prayer points

- Pray for the fruit of the Holy Spirit in your life
- Pray against the spirit of wasted emotions in Jesus name

- Pray that God will help you to distinguish between healthy and unhealthy emotions in your life
- Pray that God will help you to distinguish between true love and infatuation

Amen

CHAPTER THREE

IS THIS TRUE LOVE?

This is one of the frequently asked questions among young people. Since love is highly associated with deep good feelings, they want to know how to be sure of what they feel whether it is true love or not.

Below are six facts about true love.

1. *True love accepts weakness*

   An unknown author once said, "People we love in our lives are like pillars on our porch. Sometimes they hold us up and sometimes they lean on us, sometimes it's just enough to know they are standing by." Human beings are mortal and mortality restricts them from being faultless. No human being is without faults. If you are going to look for blameless, pure love, you will never find it in human beings. You must express some willingness to understand even when you are sure of the others' weaknesses.

In short, true love accepts people for who they are. Nevertheless, accepting people for who they are does not mean we should condone gross behavior. If your partner's weakness leads you to sin, seek external counsel from a godly mature couple and if the problem persists even after being counseled, end the relationship.

When two people in a relationship admit their weaknesses and express a willingness to change, their weaknesses are turned to strengths. Willingness to change overpowers weaknesses.

A very close friend of mine had problems with his fiancée and was about to quit so he came to ask for advice from me. After a long discussion on phone over the issue I told him something that challenged his thinking about what we were discussing and later it also influenced my way of thinking about love and relationships. After he outlined for me a long list of the weaknesses of the lady, I told him that Jesus did not choose Judas after he betrayed him. He chose him before the betrayal. Meaning that, we should not solely use the reasons of disappointment and betrayal to reject our partners even when they are sorry for what they have done.

2. *Do you really care?*

How often do you hear yourself say, "I don't care," "Who cares?" etc. if you find it easy to say such words, you are not in love because true love cares and you must care. It's not an option; care is every person's need. Care instills a sense of acceptance in the heart of a person. Rejection is the absence of care. Therefore, if you really love your partner, you must care.

- When the spiritual life of your partner seems to be dying, you must care.
- When your partner is in trouble, you must care.
- When your partner's performance in his/her day to day affairs dwindles e.g. commitment to goals goes down, you must care.

Someone said, "People don't care how much you know until they know how much you care."

3. *What is your interest in that person?*

Infatuation, commonly known as love at first sight is a serious problem among young people. In fact, if we are to critically look at infatuation for what it is, we are wrong to define it is as "love at first sight" but would be correct to say that it is strong emotional feelings mistaken for love for someone. You also have to realize that infatuation is not just 'love at first sight'. You can be infatuated over someone you know very well.

True love however, has good interests in another person. Being strongly attracted to a person for their looks or what they do is a deadly vice in your love life. What is it that interests you about the person you say you love? Is it their voice, body structure, complexion, job or what?

If your interest is not more in the character of the person you say you love, there is a problem. Body structure changes, I know some sisters and brothers who were slim and over the years they have bulged. They are fat! Complexions can change with a change of environment. I have also known people whose complexion has changed because they were accidentally burned. In short, these outward attractions can change overnight and therefore, you need to be more attracted to a person's character than the mere outward appearance.

If the physical appearance of the person you say you love changed overnight, could you still be willing to be with him/her? Could you still feel the same way about them emotionally? If she lost those eyes that captivate you, could you still be happy to love a blind girl? For ladies, over the physical appearance of that man that enchants you; if he lost one of his legs; would you still proudly introduce him to your friend or family?

4. *Love must be defined*

You cannot say "I just love you and I don't know why?" you must know why you love that person. Think of your favorite fruit or drink, if asked why you like it so much you will be able to describe it. This should be the same with love. You must be able to pinpoint why you love somebody.

A common problem among young people and those intending to be in relationships is that, they get carried away by the deeds of a person other than who the person really is in terms of their character.

Do you love the person for who they are or for what they do or have?
Do you love the preaching?
Do you love the job?
Do you love the dressing taste?
Do you love the car or what? Tell us! You say you know better but can't just explain. If you can't explain it then you don't know period.
True love must be directed at, and motivated by the good traits in the personality of someone and not what the person does. What is your definition of true love?

5. *The 'Fill in the Blank' Test*
When people fall in love, they often want to spend their forever together. A long absence of a loved one instills in us feelings of loneliness and void. But what do you do when your loved one is not around- When you are miles apart? Do you

decide to fill up the emptiness in the company of another person? Do you find yourself assuming that is what the other person could be doing?

True love never justifies unfaithfulness. John Mason says "love will find a way; everything else will find an excuse".

Do you bother to stay in touch or you say he or she will communicate anytime he or she feels like? What do you do to fill up the "miss you" feeling? Love is faithfulness.

One of the major tests of true love is distance. Many people have argued that distance relationships hardly work and to an extent it is a fact but the question is why? Why do distance relationships seldom work? It is because relationships call for commitment and many people are not ready to commit themselves to relationships. No matter the distance between two hearts that have genuinely resolved to love each other, they will still beat as one. True love knows no distance.

6. *Love Must Be Expressed*

Love must be expressed and not just talked about. It is one thing to say you love a person and it is another to demonstrate your love in action. God did not just say he loved us; he gave up His one and only Son as a demonstration of love for us.

My wife, then my fiancée always complained that I just said I loved her but never demonstrated it. I truly loved and still love her now as my wife but I never knew how to show it so I had to learn her. I had to understand what her definition of love was and I had to start doing what she enjoyed seeing me do for her. I think the key thing is to learn your partners' needs and making efforts to meet them. I highly recommend the book "the five languages of love" written by Gary Chapman for a better understanding of this very important point.

True love is defined by the extent of one's willing to demonstrate it through sacrifice in two ways:

Self-sacrifice

This is ones willingness to give himself or herself totally to the partner under what circumstances. Self-sacrifice puts one's self on the line. You would take the bullet before it hits him or her. When exchanging marriage vows it is locked in phrases like "for better or worse, for richer or poorer...... until death do us part." Don't play with love; it calls for demonstration by self-sacrifice.

Possession sacrifice

This is ones willingness to share all of his or her worldly goods. If you are too selfish to share what you have with another, forget about being involved in any sensible love relationship. In marriage vows there is a line selfish people don't want to hear and if they had a way they would have plucked it out from the pages of the marriage vows. It says "all my worldly goods I share with you".

Prayer points

- Lord teach me to truly and selflessly love

- lord teach me to appreciate love form others

- lord teach me to forgive just as I would like to be forgiven

CHAPTER FOUR

WAYS LOVE CAN BE EXPRESSED

Love must not just be talked about but must be expressed. Many people are good at discussing love but practicing it is far from them. Below are ways you can express love.

Learn to be a giver

True love gives. 'I love you' notes or SMS'; A phone call just to check on your partner, birthday cards, flowers; chocolate etc. whatever gift may suit the occasion, give gifts to your partner. Do not just be a recipient of gifts but a giver as well. Do something special for someone you love and treat them out on things they enjoy.

Give support to your partner

Every human being desires to be supported in what they do. Whatever concerns your partner, do your best to support him or her. Of course the support you give must be on things that are helping your partner to succeed in their pursuits in life and these things are not harmful to their spiritual, physical, and emotional life. You cannot support your partner if they are planning to go hung themselves.

There is no joy that can be compared to that of knowing that your partner is behind you as you pursue your dreams. A story is told of a man who lost all he worked for in a fire and people came to sympathize with him but he told them not to because he still had his wife and kids by his side. "I haven't lost it all; I still have my wife and kids by my side." He said.

Be concerned over your partner
It is often so inspiring to know that someone is concerned over your wellbeing. Be concerned over your partners' well-being. When things are not working well for your partner be concerned. When you are concerned over your partners wellbeing and he or she notices it, they will be happy to share their deepest needs and desires with you and that will draw you closer in your relationship. Openness in a relationship is enhanced when partners show genuine concern for each other.

Give attention to your partner
Never be too busy for your partner. So many times you can be so occupied with your own things failing to give time to the people we love. One of the pastors I know Carol kiyakilika narrated a story of a man who preferred to spend time at some bar because according to him at home his wife never gave him any attention. He actually claimed she could easily recognize a dog when it walked in the house than when he did.

There is nothing as harmful as being ignored by your partner in a relationship.

Nine ways you can pay attention:

Learn to listen and not just to hear.
We hear with our ears but we listen with our hearts. In short take to heart what your partner is saying. Never say it is a small matter that needs no worry at all. To your partner it is a huge thing that needs your attention. The greatest desire of every human being is to find a close friend that is ready to listen.

Proper posture

Whenever your partner seeks your attention, give it to them by stopping whatever you are going and face them. Give undivided attention to your partner by offering a seat and let them see it in your body posture that they are not wasting your time. When your partner has asked for your time, avoid talking to them while standing. Standing suggests that you are in a hurry so the speaker must say whatever they want to say quickly.

Eye contact

Look at your partner when he or she is talking to you. Avoid looking somewhere else when your partner is talking to you. Excuse yourself if you have been distracted by something.

Learn to give

No matter how little your resources are, learn to share. Gifts given with a right motive speak volumes to the receiver. It is an expression of value and care. It means you are thoughtful of the other person.

Learn to appreciate effort
No matter how insignificant the effort may appear to be in your eyes learn to appreciate it. You don't know what it took for him or her to do what they have done. Never despise effort.

Keep records of special events
Keep records of major events in your partner's life. Know your partners family, friends and under what circumstances never forget their birthdays. Memorize names of your partner's friend and her family members. It is not dullness when you record such details in your diary.

On one of my birthdays, my wife bought me a pair of shoes, a shirt and some socks. Wow!!!!!!!!!!! I felt loved!

Be thankful.
Failure to say thank you to your partner for what they have done for you, implies you do not appreciate his or her effort and whatever he or she is doing is none of your business. Never take your partners kindness for granted they may not always be there to show it one day.

Learn to say sorry

You are not an angel. You are a fallible human being. You make mistakes. Don't be big headed. C.S Lewis once said, "There is nothing progressive about being big headed and refusing to admit a mistake." Say sorry when you are wrong. Don't just buy an expensive gift, say it. Say "sorry I was wrong" and ask for forgiveness.

Admit ignorance on some issues.

When you don't know something, don't try to pretend as if you do know it all. Learn from your partner. In fact never marry a person from whom you cannot learn anything. There is an old local saying from the Eastern part of our country that says "safunsa anadya pula" meaning the man that was too proud to admit ignorance on the difference between honey and wax, ended up eating wax leaving the honey itself. Be humble enough to say "I don't know."

Prayer points
- Lord teach me not only to love with words but deeds also
- Lord, my heart is open and ready to be loved

Amen

CHAPTER FIVE

REASONS WHY SOME RELATIONSHIPS DON'T WORK

Even after investing so much time, money and love in a relationship, most of them don't work. Their end is usually disastrous. Two love birds that started their relationship with such flavor and deep romantic feelings end up in bitter hostility and hatred. The obvious question that many people will ask is "what went wrong?" how could such a beautiful beginning of a love story end up into a sad story?

I liken the journey of love to driving on a road you have never driven on before. Often you will not know how your journey will be like. You may find several road blocks to stop you, road humps to slow you, detours to delay you, dusty roads, depressions to overwhelm you, and breakdowns to stop your journey. When you go through some of these things, you have several options to choose from. You can either decide to abandon the journey or go on after fixing the problem you have encountered. Fixing the problem may not be that easy but with commitment and dedication to reach your destination, you can manage to find a way of having the job done.

It is the process of fixing problems that cause many people to choose to give up and throw in the towel. Below are suggested reasons of why some relationships don't work:

Weak foundation
It is common knowledge that the strength of a building is determined by the nature of its foundation.

This is true of relationships. How you start your relationship determines the kind of foundation that you will lay for it and it is on that foundation that your relationship will be built.

Settle it in your mind that every relationship no matter how sweet it starts, will face its share of the challenges that come as a result of two people coming from different backgrounds. External and internal storms will beat against your relationship and if your foundation is weak that will mark the end of your relationship.

Some characteristics of a weak foundation:

- Relationships started in a haste
- Wrong reasons for entering into a relationship e.g. sex
- Relationship motivated by material possessions e.g. a car
- Relationship started through betrayal of a friend or partner
- Relationship started with sexual compromise

Distrust

When two people in a relationship cannot trust each other anymore that usually marks the beginning of the end of that relationship. Trust is the backbone of a relationship. Trust is the life line of a relationship. It is the power source of a relationship. If you don't trust the person you are in a relationship with, it will not last. You will do everything possible to keep away from him or her. You will zip your mouth from saying anything sensitive in their presence. A relationship coated with distrust is headed for a destructive end.

Unrealistic expectation

Any normal human being will expect something positive to come out of all the decisions they make and relationship decisions are none excluded. When people enter relationships, they enter with expectations and it is okay. But the expectations certain people have in relationships are farfetched dreams that could never come to pass whether here on earth or on planet mars! To expect a good wedding is a very good thing but to expect one where you will have a convoy of hammers is unacceptable when you know you do not have enough money for such a wedding.

You also don't expect your partner to be an angel who never goes wrong. I have bad news for you, whoever he or she is, they will do you wrong at times. So do not expect them to be angels.

Unrealistic expectations in relationship will breed unnecessary conflicts that may lead to its end.

Pre-marital sex

Sex outside marriage has had impressive records of breaking solid relationships into pieces. Any time people have premarital sex; seeds of distrust feeling of uneasiness, anxiety and betrayal are unconsciously planted. It may seem as if sex has strengthened a relationship but sooner than later, trouble will erupt from nowhere and you will fail to understand why and how things have turned sour. Premarital sex kills relationships. If you get into such a marriage, with that kind of background, without proper counsel and prayer, your marriage will be hell on earth.

Do your best to resist sexual involvement before you marry?

Premarital sex will make the lady feel used and the man will suddenly lose interest in her. She will lose the sense of self-respect and the man will not respect her anymore. She will stop trusting the man and the man will stop trusting her as well. Fears of unwanted pregnancies will trouble both the man and the lady. Above all, for Christians they will both have feelings of guilt and condemnation.

Negative External views of your relationship
Some people will have negative views of your relationship. They will do and say things to discredit your relationship. Have your own definition of your

own relationship because if you don't, people will define it for you.

Negative Internal views of your relationship
When you begin to think your relationship is useless, sheer waste of time, it will fail to work. Have a right perception of your relationship. A right perception of your relationship gives value to your relationship. A bad perception of your relationship will lead to the sad end of your relationship.

Family acceptance
If the family of your partner cannot accept him or her, it will lead to failure of your relationship. Who would want to marry from a family that hates him or her? Never give a blind eye to negative attitudes of family members to your relationship. If it will take prayer and fasting to change negative attitudes of family members to your relationship, do it now. Do whatever it takes to win the approval of your family of your relationship.

Failure to believe in your partner
When you cannot believe in your partner's dreams, they will soon notice it and grow cold towards you.

Below are suggested ways a relationship can work:

- *Let your relationship be founded on prayer and Gods word*
  Prayer and Gods word will give a very strong foundation for your relationship.

- *The fear of God*
  Fear God in your relationship. Keep sin away in your relationship. In particular do everything possible to avoid immoral conduct in your relationship.

- *Never enter into a relationship with someone you don't trust*
  Learn to trust your partner and be trust worthy yourself.

- *Avoid negative views of people about your relationship*
  Never believe rumors about your relationship until the truth is clearly established. People are entitled to their own opinion so don't allow that to be so much a bother to you.

- *Be enthusiastic about your relationship*
  Believe and be convinced that your relationship is one of the best in town. Be proud of your relationship. When everyone says negative things

about relationships, always use the success of your relationship as a positive example.

- *Pray for acceptance in your families*
Trust God that your family will not develop a negative attitude towards your partner and love your partner's family and accept them as they are. Some may really get on your nerves but love them. Be tolerant and sensitive to their needs. You do not want them to gung up against you because you are not in good boots with them.

- *Believe in your partners dreams.*
Let him or her know that they are the best for whatever they are doing. All humans fall in love with people who believe in their potential and capabilities. Encourage your partner to pursue his or her dreams.

Even God, He only does wonders when we believe in Him.

Prayer points

- Lord, let the foundation of my love life be repaired in Jesus' name

- My love life shall not be a disaster
- All foundational powers from my past working against my love life I reject your effect on me in the name of Jesus

Amen

CHAPTER SIX

HOW TO RECOGNISE THE GOD SENT PARTNER IN YOUR LIFE

For many single Christians, the idea of marrying a person sent from God is a daily desire.

No one wants to marry a wrong partner in life. Unless you are mad. Marrying a wrong partner in life is detrimental to one's destiny. So every Christian believer wants to marry a God sent man or woman. Below are ways you can recognize a God sent marriage partner:

He or she may not look like what you have been dreaming about.

Many young people that are ready for marriage have missed their God sent partners because of preconceived idea of Gods ideal man or woman for them. Even in the bible many people missed God because they expected God to do things their way. Don't be glued to that long list of qualities of a man or woman who does not exist. Pray to God to open your eyes to recognize your God sent man or woman in your life. You may say "well God gives us the desires of our hearts." It is true but only when we delight ourselves in him. When we delight ourselves in him, we will have desires that are aligned with his will for our lives. Of course you wouldn't want to marry someone whom you don't admire physically but let God help you to choose the right one among the good looking guys or girls you are looking at. Not every good looking person is a suitable partner for you. There are also good looking devils around.

He or she may not say what you always want to hear
A God sent man or woman will tell you the truth about their social status and background. They will not cook unfounded stories of themselves. Crooked men and women can lie just to have a piece of your life to them and afterwards evaporate into the unknown. Be very careful how you treat a man or woman who gives you a genuine story of their life. He or she may be the God sent man in your life.

There are people who are always talking about what their parents own. Which part of the city they come from- What kind of car they will be driving in the next month and so forth. They have nothing substantial to talk about. Their tongues are full of 'I's and 'ME's'. Be very careful with such kind of characters.

He or she is interested in your spiritual, physical and social life.
A genuine God sent partner will be interested in your wellbeing spiritually, physically and socially. He or she will have your interest at heart. He or she will be there to give advice and counsel that will advance you in life. When you meet a man or woman who genuinely pushes you to pursue your God given assignment in life, he or she could be a God sent partner in your life.

He or she is a spiritual person.
A God sent partner is a person that fears God. He or she is a prayerful person. A man or woman who doesn't pray but plays will make you his or her prey.
A God sent partner also reads and knows his or her bible well. If not that well, he or she will show genuine interest in knowing the bible. He or she

loves seeing you at Christian gatherings and delights in seeing you grow spiritually. If a man or woman keeps you away from spiritual activities such as prayer, reading the bible, going to church, reading spiritual books etc., he or she is from the devil.

He or she has nothing to hide
A God sent partner will give clear intentions of what they are looking for in the relationship. He or she will openly tell you his or her interest in the relationship. If someone interested in you seems to be unsure of where the relationship is going, run for your heart. Before a person proposes or says yes to a proposal for a relationship, they must be sure of what they are getting into.

He or she is comfortable serving God with you.
A man or woman sent by God will be free to worship God with you. He will be free to evangelize, pray and study the Bible with you. A man or woman who refuses to serve God with you has very dangerous intentions against you. I as a young pastor have seen many fellow young people that were on fire for Jesus become ice cold spiritually because

they started dating some funny character who kept them away from church.

You could be saying this church-staff is not what I bought this book for. Well sorry to let you know that this church staff is what this book is all about.

A God sent man or woman prays with you.
A man or woman who refuses to pray with you is a very dangerous man. If a man or woman cannot pray with you, run for your life. Through prayer we draw closer to God so what business should you have with a person that does not want to get close to God with you?

A God sent man or woman corrects you.
A man or woman who has courage to rebuke you regardless of what your reaction could be the God sent partner in your life. A man from the devil will not risk questioning your wrongs for fear of being rejected.
A God sent man or woman inspires you spiritually, socially and morally.

A God sent man will inspire you spiritually, socially and morally. If a person does not inspire you in these areas, run for your life fast!

A God sent man or woman must be born again
Never be fooled to think God can bring a non-believer to marry you. If a person you want to get into a relationship with has a questionable testimony of salvation, never give in to their sweet charm of love stories. The Bible says, "Do not be yoked together with unbelievers. For what do righteousness and wickedness have in common? How can light live with darkness? What harmony is there between Christ and Belial? Or what does a believer have in common with an unbeliever? 2 Corinthians 6:14-15.

I guess the scripture above is as clear as the blue sky. God says don't do it. Don't marry a non believer. In His wisdom, knowing all things including hearts of men, God your father in heaven commands us to have nothing to do with none believers when it comes to falling in love. You don't want the devil for a father in law, do you?

Prayer point

- My eyes open to identify my God sent love partner in the name of Jesus
- My heart you shall not miss your match in the name of Jesus
- With the eyes of faith, I will identify the love of my life in the name of Jesus
- I shall not love the wrong person in the name of Jesus
- My God sent partner, appear without delay in the name of Jesus

Amen

CHAPTER SEVEN

BEING FRIENDS BEFORE LOVERS

Friendship is one of the major keys to building healthy and long lasting relationships. If you cannot be my friend, you can not be my lover period.

Many young people are misled to think a relationship is all about romance- sex. Well, in the first place it should not be at all. Sex is meant to be enjoyed in marriage but even marriage is not all about sex. Believe me its not. Without friendship, it's boring to fall in love. Being in a relationship without friendship is like having a cell phone without network connection. You just can not connect. Every time you attempt to love someone who is not your friend, you would be getting a message like this " The heart you are trying to love is outside the romantic coverage area or has their emotions switched off please don't waste your precious time!"

Reasons why you should be friends before lovers;

1. Friends accept us for who we are:
   Friends accept us for who we are and that is what true love should be about, accepting each other for who we are. If anyone claims to love you, he or she must be able to accept you for who you are. I have different kinds of friends. They are all unique physically and they have different temperaments but they are my friends and I have accepted them for who they are. That is how a relationship must be also.
2. We are more real with friends than lovers:
   When you love someone, you will do everything possible to please them. You may even borrow clothes to create an impression but with a friend you are more honest and realistic because there is nothing to prove to your friend.
3. With a friend, moments of pretence are usually low:
   A friend usually has nothing to prove. They know that you like them as they are and when unhappy they will not pretend to please you.
4. It is in friendship that you discover things in common:

You wouldn't love to be in a relationship with a man or woman who is totally the opposite of what you are. In true friendship, there must be a certain level of commonality of interests.

5. Most romantic stories were founded on long time friendship:

   Best of lovers in town were once good friends. Some met in high school, some on the bus to another city, some at church, some met during some sport outing or wherever but they became good friends and ended up in fruitful relationships.

6. A friend will protect your reputation:

   Real friends will be there to protect your reputation when it's endangered and you wouldn't want to be in a relationship with a man or woman who cannot protect your name. When people are speaking ill of you in the presence of your friend should they dare, your friend will strongly defend you.

7. A real friend believes in your dreams:

   As a person that wants to accomplish something positive on earth, you want a lover who will believe in your dreams. In real friendship, people always have faith in each other's dreams. I have a friend Gideon K Chibwe, he is a pastor with wild dreams but I believe in them. One of his dreams is to be a father of triplets! I will not go to him and say it cannot be done and if we will have to try them out together I will be there to support him. Of course I can't help him in anyway over the triplet's issue it's his job!

8. We are usually proud of friends

I have never seen a real friendship were people involved are ashamed of each other. No matter the physical disposition of a friend, you are always proud of them and you wouldn't want to be in a relationship with someone that thinks you are ugly and mad. Pastor Gideon K Chibwe has always been shorter than me and I like him for that!

9. A real friend is interested in your well being

A real friend does not look out only for what they can get out of you but what they can invest in you. You don't want to be in a relationship with a person who only wants to suck goodness from you and never adding anything to your life.

10. Real friends will be free to disagree with you

A real friend will sometimes disagree with you and you will disagree with them. Sometimes the

disagreements can be so sharp such that one would wander whether you would ever reconcile but somehow, you get over your misunderstanding and your friendship continues.
I believe true love has to have components of misunderstandings and sometimes sharp disagreements. If you are able to resolve sharp conflicts in your friendship, then your relationship will last long.

Prayer points:

- Lord teach me to be genuinely friendly to the opposite sex in Jesus name

- Lord let my life attract genuine opposite sex friends in Jesus name

- Lord I refuse to live a life full of pretence in the name of Jesus

- Lord teach me to be humble in the name of Jesus

Amen

CHAPTER EIGHT

DANGERS OF PREMARITAL SEX

Sex is Gods design. Sex is not evil. It is good and meant to be practiced within the confine of a marriage. These days, sex is no longer viewed as sacred. People practice sex at will outside the morally acceptable decrees of the Bible. But the consequences of premarital sex are fatal. The damage it can cause to a relationship can be irreparable if not given immediate spiritual attention and counsel. I know to some people this may sound old but the truth is that there is no joy in having sex with someone that is not your spouse. Some people even move in to live together before marriage. They live like husband and wife but the end of such relationships is very sad and painful as earlier noted when I wrote about cohabiting. Resist the temptation of having sex with a person you have not exchanged vows with. Don't!

Seven reasons to avoid premarital sex

Based on the Bible passage of 1 Corinthians 6:15-20 we deduce some reasons why you and your partner should avoid premarital sex:

The scripture says:
Do you not know that your bodies are members of Christ? Shall I then take the members of Christ and make them members of a harlot? Certainly not! Or do you not know that he who is joined to a harlot is one body with her? For "the two" he says, "shall become one flesh." But he who is joined to the Lord is one spirit with Him.

Flee sexual immorality. Every sin that a man does is outside the body, but he who commits sexual immorality sins against His own body.

Or do you not know that your body is the temple of the Holy Spirit who is in you, who you have from God, and you are not your own? For you were bought at a price: therefore, glorify God in your body and in your spirit which are God's. (NKGV)
Your body belongs to the lord Jesus

This means you cannot indulge your body in activities that offend Jesus the owner of your body. It is not for His good that God has said you should not commit fornication. It is for your good.

You become one with anyone you sexually involve yourself with.

This is not my idea. It is Gods. It implies that you will share in the personality of the one you sexually involve yourself with. "The two, shall become one."

Everything that your partner is, you become.
Many people have wandered how suddenly some things in their lives suddenly took a certain course. They hardly realize that it can be attributed to the fact that they had sex with someone with the exact life pattern.

Sexual sin is sinning against your self
As opposed to other sins, when you sin sexually, it is against yourself. In short it is committing an offence against your-self. It means hurting yourself and often it is very hard to forgive yourself. When one person hurts you, you can decide to do away with them but

when you offend yourself, you can't do away with yourself. Imagine trying to run away from yourself. Your body is the temple of the Holy Spirit

Remember He is called the "holy spirit" this means he has no business with ungodly living. Sexual sin grieves the Holy Spirit and makes Him unhappy with the one that commit it.

Your life is costly
Jesus had to die for you to have eternal life. He paid for your sins even before you practically committed them. He actually did not have your sins forgiven on credit; He paid the cost for your sin in full. The total cost was paid for your salvation. Jesus died for you to have your sins forgiven so please honor Him with your body.

The other reasons why you should not engage yourself in sexual immorality not deduced from the above quoted scripture are that:

You can attract sexually transmitted diseases.
In this age of immorality, it is not easy to determine how many sexual practices your partner has been

involved in. you can get a sexually transmitted disease that can end in death.

You can attract unexpected pregnancy
Many young people have wrecked their careers because a sexual involvement resulted in unexpected pregnancy. For Christians, their lives are on a hill top and many people are watching their life without them noticing. Pregnancies outside the wedlock, often brings disgrace to the body of Christ. You also could not be ready to take up the responsibility of parenting.

Prayer points:

- Lord, forgive me for any sexual sins whether by thoughts or the actual act. Please lord, have mercy on me and cleans me with the precious blood of Jesus. Purify me of any spiritual contamination and help me to live a pure life in the name of Jesus.

- Lord Jesus give me a new start with you and give me the wisdom to flee every appearance of evil in the name of Jesus

CHAPTER NINE

FIVE PRACTICAL STEPS TO AVOID SEXUAL SIN

Avoid sexual chatting

Fantasizing about a sexual experience with your partner will plant seeds for the actual act. Never be fooled, you are a saved spirit living in a biological body. When you engage in sexual fantasies, messages are sent to your brain which releases some hormones to prepare you for the action. For heaven's sake, talk about bananas and mangoes with your partner. I think this sound like Holy romance!

Avoid long time body contact

Do not fool yourself and do not let anyone fool you. There is a big difference in the physical make up between male and female. Spending long time body contact with your partner is not wisdom but foolishness. When a man's body gets close to that of a lady, there will usually be a reaction. The bodies will begin to react. You will begin to have tender feelings of sexual attraction and before you know it you will find yourselves laying hands on each other.

I have deliberately used the expression 'long time' because body language such as short hugs or holding hands are an important component in a relationship. But long time, cozy hugs, kissing, and cuddling in a dark room or in a banana plantation, are recipes for sexual immorality for the unmarried. I wholeheartedly advise you to be careful and mindful how close you will get to your partner physically.

Take time to pray together for purity in your relationship
The devil hates to see two love birds praying together. He enjoys it when he sees you compromising in your relationship. He enjoys it when you sin not when you pray. Develop a habit of praying together in your relationship for purity. Never buy into the carnal idea that praying together with your partner in your relationship is being over spiritual. That is the devils idea. In fact, you relationship must be spiritualized and not made carnal. It may not be a one hour prayer session but even a minute of praying together with your partner is a hurtful thing to the devil that would rather see you sinning. This godly practice will bring a sense of Godly fear in your relationship.

Note that we will discuss in depth the component of prayer in relationships because I believe that prayer is vital for any Christian relationship.

Take time as an individual to pray for your relationship:
Praying for your relationship as an individual is a sign that you treasure it and you want Gods best for it. It is also an individual expression of your trust in God for the success of your relationship. This also builds your personal relationship with God which results into a sense of godly fear and holiness.
Soak yourselves in God's word

Develop a habit of studying the Bible together.
Memorize scripture, recite them to each other once in a while, and share something new that has impressed you from your personal bible studies with your partner. The psalmist in the bible book of Psalm 119:9 asked a question that he had an answer to when he said:
How can a young person keep his life pure? He can do it by holding on to your word. (God's word translation)

If you can make time to feed each other ice cream, go see a movie, swimming or any other romantic events to spice up your relationship, shouldn't you make time for God's word together? I think a logical answer is that you should. You must make time for God's word together.

If you and your partner have been indulging in sex, resolve to stop. Talk about it and let there be a mutual agreement that it is sin and it displeases God and thus must be stopped. You can take a further step of seeing a spiritually mature Christian for prayer and counseling.

Below are some practical steps you can take to deal with sexual sin in your relationship:

a) Acknowledge that you have been living in sin and ask God in the name of Jesus to forgive you for the sexual sins you have committed. There is no Sin that Jesus cannot forgive.

b) Ask Jesus to clean your mind from moral contamination.

c) Renounce any soul ties created as a result of the act of sexual immorality.

d) Expel by faith any demon or immoral spirit that might have entered your life as a result of you involving yourself in sexual immorality.

e) Do away with any object or obscene material that would increase chances of you going back to your old life style of sexual immorality.

f) Ask the Holy Spirit to take total control of your life.

g) By faith thank God for your deliverance.

h) Actions to take following your deliverance:

- Break the relationship if your partner is not a believer in Jesus. That is if he or she is not born again. Don't cheat yourself that you will change him or her. You won't and you can't. Only God changes people

- Destroy any sexually arousing material by physical fire in Jesus name. E.g. pornographic material and if you have been browsing on the internet for such, make a resolve to discontinue.

- Break out from any friendship with people who do not share in your new path whether they may be close friends. The bible warns in 1 Corinthians 15:33;

Do not be deceived; evil companionships corrupt good habits. (NKJV)

- Look for good Christian books and sermon topics on purity, holiness in relationship and other related books to continue growing in knowledge as you pursue a holy life.
- Avoid worldly music and movies that will arouse your sexual desires.

Prayer points:

- Lord give me the grace to stay away from every appearance of evil in the name of Jesus
- I will not fall in any demonic trap to fall into sexual immorality in the name of Jesus
- My body is the temple of the holy spirit and I will not defile it through illicit sex in the name of Jesus
- My body is not a candidate for the invasion of the spirits of lust in the name of Jesus. Amen

CHAPTER TEN

PRAYING TOGETHER IN YOUR RELATIONSHIP

Praying together is usually a less likely activity in relationships. People in relationships are usually clouded by romantic feelings for each other such that it is considered old to talk about prayer in their relationship but prayer, is a very important component if a relationship will be built on the principles of God's word.

- Pray together to raise a prayer altar for your present and future

- Although I am not writing on prayer, the power of prayer in a relationship cannot be undermined. The spiritual character of your relationship is what you will carry into your marriage. Praying together in your relationship will lay a strong, good and godly foundation for a lifelong relationship.

- Pray together to proclaim mutual dependence on God.

- Your relationship needs God. Without God, you cannot live a fulfilled love life. Human beings are selfish by nature. It takes God to transform the mind of people for them to be thoughtful of others. When we pray, we become aware of the other person because God enables us to genuinely love and care for others.
- Pray because the devil is not happy to see you in a happy relationship.
- Believe me; the devil will not sit having a glass of juice while seeing you enjoying a happy love life. He will come after you with all that he can to bring misery and pain in your relationship but praying together will create an atmosphere of mutual spiritual cover over your relationship.
- Pray together as a proclamation of oneness in faith.
- You never planned to marry a Buddhist or a Muslim or a person from any other religion apart from Christianity. Praying together is a sign of mutual proclamation of your faith in Jesus. You do not want to wake up one Monday morning only to hear your partner telling you that they

belong to a faith whose beliefs you do not believe.

- Pray together because God promises to answer your prayers when you pray in agreement.
- If two of you shall agree as touching anything on earth, it shall be agreed upon in heaven.
- Pray together because prayer promotes holiness in a relationship.
- It is in the time of prayer that we get to see our imperfections-We see our sins, our inadequacies and failures. As you pray together, God will be revealing areas in your life where you need to change.
- Prayer draws you closer to each other.
- As you pray together, you draw near to each other as you draw near to God. As shown in the triangle below:

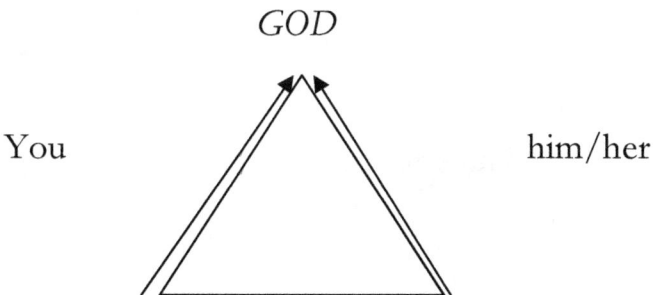

GOD

You   him/her

The arrows represent you and your partner. The closer you get to God, the closer you get to each other. The opposite is also true that when you get further away from God, the further you will get from each other.

Prayer points:

- Lord Jesus baptize our relationship with fresh fire to pray in the name of Jesus

- Let our relationship be founded on the foundation of prayer in the name of Jesus

- Lord Jesus, give me and my partner the grace to value prayer in the name of Jesus

- Every power of worldliness opposing our desire to pray in our relationship I reject you in the name of Jesus

CHAPTER ELEVEN

THE IMPORTANCE OF MENTORSHIP IN YOUR RELATIONSHIP

One of the key ingredients that would make your relationship work is having a couple you can look up to for mentorship. A mentor is someone you look up to for inspiration and counsel. He or she is a person with whom you will be willing to share not only your fears but also your joys. He is a person that has gone ahead of you in the area of life where you are pursuing success.

For you to be successful in your relationship, you may need a couple that you can look up to for advice and inspiration. Below are eight reasons why you should seriously consider finding a relationship mentor.

1. For accountability's sake
For a relationship to be successful there is need to be accountable. Accountability instills a sense of responsibility in your relationship. You need an authority figure to speak into your relationship. This

is a good approach to avoid unnecessary breakups in relationships. People sometimes end relationships due to funny reasons but when you are accountable you will be required to give a convincing reason for ending a relationship.

2. *For confidentiality*
Relationship go through a lot of challenges and you will need someone especially a married couple that you can open up to and share your deepest concerns, fears and anxieties; even failures. You don't have to go about publicizing to the world the challenges in your relationships. You can find a good couple for mentorship and pour your hearts to them.

3. *For reality check up*
Someone said "love is blind" this implies that when two people are in love, they live in a world of their own outside reality. It is a world where only the two of them exist. It is often a world of wishful thinking, fantasy and unrealistic desires and there is need for someone outside that world to bring the gospel of reality to the two love birds otherwise they will end

up frustrated when reality dawns on them unexpectedly.

4. *For resolving of conflicts*

A relationship involves two people coming from different backgrounds, having different perspectives about life. There will be times when the two cannot agree on some issues. A relationship mentor in such cases can be instrumental in helping the two resolve the conflict in love and understanding. Many good relationships had a sad end because of failure by the people involved to resolve their differences. They thought quitting was the only way out of the misunderstandings but the sad thing is that they never had someone to talk to before they quit.

In times of conflicts in a relationship, a mentor will often act as a neutral party to give advice that may lead to settling the dispute an amicable way.

5. *For moral support*

In any normal relationship, there will be sexual temptations. In the first place, one of the reasons you were attracted to that person is sex! "Pastor that's a lie!" dear reader, "that's a fact!" the sooner you realize this is a fact the better. You are a sexual being. Never hide your feeling in the umbrella of spirituality. You will fall. As you get deeper and deeper in love, you also get closer and closer emotionally but and also physically.

A mentor can give logical and practical advice on how you can maintain sexual purity in a relationship. They can also keep checking on you; how you are coping with sexual pressure. This will instill in you a sense of fear and accountability.

6. *For spiritual support*

There is so much joy in knowing that there is someone that is talking to God about your relationship. Every relationship needs spiritual support. If you are in a relationship or intending to get into one, you need people who can be praying for you and giving spiritual encouragement. A mentor is the best to give this kind of support because they know and understand the challenges you could be going through spiritually. They have best interest at heart for you.

7. *For motivational support*

Every relationship will have its high and low moments. Seasons of discouragements that may cause two people to give up in a relationship will come. But it is at this time that you will need someone to motivate you to hang on a little longer. A mentor will motivate you to press on, to try new ways of doing things and handling of issues in your relationship. A mentor will motivate you.

8. *For inspiration*

We all have some people we admire and look up to for inspiration in different areas of our lives. Your relationship needs a good marriage to inspire you, to show you that it is very possible to have a good and happy marriage. Your mentor should be a source of inspiration in this regard.

It is very difficult to find inspiring marriages in these days. Marriages have become so fragile and many are breaking up. Such scenarios can instill fears and uncertainties in the minds and hearts of young people pursuing a marriage relationship but your mentor's happy marriage can inspire you to look forward to a happy marriage in your future.

Four things you should not expect from or about your relationship mentor(s):

I. Do not expect your mentor(s) to be a perfect

Your mentor is not an angel on earth. They are human beings like you that have just gone ahead of you in the area of relationship but they are not perfect. They may sometimes make mistakes, disappoint you or hurt you with their words or deeds but give them a benefit of doubt.

II. Do not expect your mentor(s) to support everything you do

A good mentor will not always support everything you do. Sometimes they will advice you against your wishes and desires. They could be right or wrong but don't just expect them to support all that you do.

III. Do not expect your mentors to meet all your needs

A mentor will not have answers to all your problems. Never expect your mentor to be the savior of your relationship. They are as limited as you are in how far they can assist you to meeting certain needs in your relationship.

IV. Do not expect your mentor(s) to carry out your responsibilities

You are responsible for your relationship. You started it the two of you with your partner so don't expect your mentor to be responsible for the success of your relationship. Your mentor will not love your partner on your behalf; they will not be there to make decision for you. They are there to advice and support you in any way they can but not to live the relationship for you. Take responsibility.

Prayer point

- Lord help me and my partner to find a godly couple to mentor our relationship in the name of Jesus

- Lord help us to find a couple that will have our interest at heart in the name of Jesus

- Help us oh lord to find a couple that will inspire us unto holiness in the name of Jesus

- Help us oh God to find a couple that we will be willing to submit to in the name of Jesus

Amen

CHAPTER TWELVE

TEN CHARACTERISTICS OF A GOOD RELATIONSHIP MENTOR

In the previous chapter, we looked at the need of having a relationship mentor for you to succeed in your relationship. This chapter is dedicated at showing you the basic but very important things you must look for as you search for a relationship mentor.

- The mentor(s) must be born again.

As Christians in a relationship, you need a mentor that will uphold Christian values as they provide mentorship for your relationship. Your mentor must have a genuine testimony of their faith in Jesus.

- The mentor(s) must have a good marriage testimony

You cannot be mentored by people with a bad marriage testimony. If a couple has unresolved records of physically abusing each other, extra marital affairs, bad example to their children, never make such a couple your mentor. You will receive an impartation to have a terrible marriage yourselves when you marry.

1 Corinthians 15:33 says, "Do not be deceived, bad company corrupt good morals" paraphrased

- The mentor(s) must be under a good Christian covering

You cannot be mentored by a couple that submits to a pastor whose marriage and spiritual life leaves much to be desired. Your mentor must belong to a church whose pastor is a genuine man of God that does not compromise.

- The mentor must believe in you and your relationship

You cannot have a relationship mentor who thinks you are a joker and your relationship is a disaster waiting to happen. Your mentor must be able to believe in you and your relationship.

- The mentor must have an admirable parental relationship with their children or dependants.

If a couple have literally failed to raise their children or dependants well, think twice about making them your mentor(s). There are couples that even ill-treat members of the extended family. Do not subject your relationship to that kind of anointing!

- The mentor must be hospitable

You cannot be mentored by a couple who never seem to be happy all the time you or others show up at their homes. A relationship mentor must be happy to receive you in their homes.

- The mentor must be available

A good relationship mentor will find and create time for you. You cannot be mentored by a couple that is ever busy for you. They must be available to provide the much need support as you go through the different stages of relationships.

- The mentor must inspire you with their life

You cannot be mentored by someone whose life does not inspire you- the marriage of a good relationship mentor must inspire you.

- The mentor must be able to correct you

A mentor must not fear you. They must be able to correct you when you are wrong. They must have the courage to sit you down and call you to account for some inconsistencies in your relationship and you must be willing to submit to their authority.

- The mentor must be generous

You cannot be mentored by a couple that cannot support you financially even when it is within their power to do so. A good relationship mentor must be willing to give financial support to a cause that would add value to your relationship.

How to find a good relationship mentor:

Below are five suggested means to find a good relationship mentor:

i. *Pray for a good relationship mentor*

Just as you would pray for God to guide you as you make decisions in other areas of your life, seek God concerning a good relationship mentor.

ii.   *Acknowledge the need for a relationship mentor*

Failure to acknowledge the need for a relationship mentor will result in not looking for one.

iii.   *Look for a couple you can be free with*

Never chose a couple whose presence makes you uncomfortable for mentorship. You must be free with them.

iv.   *Try to avoid distant mentorship*

The closer you are to your mentor the better the mentorship process. Chances of pretence will be slim and you will have more time to spend with your relationship mentor when they are nearby.

v.   *Look out for things that interest you in the potential mentor*

There must be things that interest you in the life of the couple you are considering to mentor your relationship especially from their marriage relationship.

Prayer points

- Lord, help us to identify a suitable relationship mentor for our relationship in the name of Jesus

- I refuse to be misled by outward appearances when choosing a relationship mentor in the name of Jesus

Amen

CHAPTER THIRTEEN

14 REASONS TO QUIT A RELATIONSHIP

It is not true that every relationship will culminate to a glorious wedding celebration. The sad thing about the pursuit of love is that we do not always succeed. We sometimes can entrust our lives with people that masquerade to be angels on earth yet they are not. What do you do when you discover that what seemed to be the ultimate love relationship turns out to be a source of pain and hurt in your life? You will have to painfully quit. Now, I can hear you silently shout "Quit?!" yes. Quit that relationship. It is painful to do so but quit. The old adage puts it right, "better a broken relationship than a broken marriage."

You have no better reason to quit that relationship than the fact that it is going nowhere. Look, you have tried whatever has to be tried but things are not getting any better. The fights are not ending, the cheating levels are increasing. The misunderstandings are unbearable. Things are just bad. You have sort advice and counsel from others but there is no change. Your partners' ways are illusive. You are not anymore sure of where your relationship is going. Quit! Yes you have built a nest around the life of that person but for heaven's sake the nest is always breaking to pieces because of the perpetual storms in that relationship. You are ever patching it up and I must guess you are tired. Quit!

You are wasting your energy by hanging on to that relationship. You are missing out on the joys of starting a whole new life. Quit! There are times when you have to quit!

Below are fourteen reasons for quitting a relationship:

1. *When you discover that your partner does not have a genuine relationship with Jesus*

No matter how long you have been in that relationship, if your partner is not a genuine follower of Jesus, you should run for your life. Quit.

Your value system cannot be the same with that of a person that professes a different faith from yours.

2. *When you discover that your partner hates your family, Quit!*

Your family is your blood line. All that you are today, your family has had a hug influence on it so how come a person can claim to be in love with you but hates your family? Quit!

3. *When you discover that your partner loves you for sex, Quit!*

Love is not just about sex. If anyone claims to love you but freaks when you guard yourself from sexual advances, Quit! They are up to no good. In fact you are not a sex object. In fact, sex outside marriage is wrong so if they insist on having it outside the boundaries of the marriage bed, cry your way out of that relationship. Quit!

4. *When you discover that your partner loves you for your money*

If a person claims to love you but is more interested in your money, Quit! Money can never buy love. What will happen when a financial crunch hit you? I will tell you what they will do; they will leave you for someone who has the money you now don't have.

5. *When you discover .that your partner is a cheater*

Some people have foolishly stayed in a relationship with a cheat in the name of love even after discovering that they are being cheated on. You are a joker! DUMP that liar before he/she does! A person who cannot be faithful in a relationship will not be faithful in a marriage.

6. *When you discover that your partner has tendencies of demeaning you.*

Your partner should be the last person to laugh at your big nose! Or whatever is funny about your looks. If your partner intimidates and demeans you, quit. It is not worth it being with such a person in a relationship.

7. *When your partner loves his/her money more than your God.*

If your partner considers his or her search for money more important than your God, Quit! Your partner must love your God as much even more than you do then you know that you are safe.

8. *When your partner loves you more than your God*

If your partner loves you more than your God, quit that relationship. You have become an idle in their life. And God hates idles and He has no good plans for idles he will destroy them.

One day I received a young good looking lady in my office. She needed prayer and counseling. Why? She married a man that loved her more than her God. Three months into her marriage, she asked me whether she made the right decision to marry him. Off course she didn't. It was a bad lifelong decision and you don't want to make it.

9. *When you are the only one making efforts to make things work in your relationship.*

You make most of the calls. You are the only one that takes trouble to visit your partner. You are always apologizing when your partner is wrong! You are the only one who remembers your partners' birthday etc. in short you are the only one that seems to care about the relationship. Quit!

10. *When your partner thinks you are ugly, quit!*

If your partner thinks you are ugly and you are still dating them, you are a fool period!

11. *When your partner is full of doubts whether you are the one or not please, Quit!*

What are you doing in that relationship for heaven's sake? It's going nowhere. Why did they take all the trouble of proposing or accepting the proposal when they were not sure? They are playing a game and you are the ball, quit!

I once got in a relationship where my girl friend told me she would only be sure whether I was the one or not after a year. Glorious heaven! I ended the relationship.

12. *When your partner is not proud to be in a relationship with you, Quit!*

Why continue in that relationship when your partner thinks you are a source of shame and disgrace? You want a partner to be proud of you.

I recently advised a sister in the lord to leave her boyfriend who had even gone ahead to propose her for marriage. She told me that he always told her that if he marries her it will be for the sake of his reputation and not his love for her. I told her to dump him, she didn't. She was scared of being single. She stayed in the horrible loveless and proud-less relationship. After a few months he dumped her. She could have done it first but he beat her at it. Shame she didn't get my advice.

13. *When your partners closest friends are non-Christian with deep questionable character traits, quit!*

If you want to know the real character of your partner, look at the persons your partner calls close friends. If your partners close friends are drunkards, cheater, and hypocrites and so forth that is what your partner is. He is a drunkard, cheater, hypocrite etc. but it is just that the hypocrisy trait has covered the other bad ones. When he marries you, you will know who he really is. This applies to ladies as well. He is a hypocrite so you cannot see that he is a crook, a cheater, a liar, a drunkard, a humaniser and a fake gem! Save your tears for other things not a broken relationship or marriage because, he will soon break your heart.

14.*When you are not ready to get married, quit that relationship.*

Why should you be in a relationship in the first place when you are not ready for marriage? Being in a relationship when you are not ready for marriage is a recipe for time wastage. I know that many young people are busy romancing each other when they are not ready for marriage. You can choose to agree or disagree with me but personal experience and those of many of my friends; as well as that of other people have proven that relationships that start without the clear cut objective of marriage have proven to be a source of devastating heartbreaks, and time wastage. In fact many relationships even among Christians that have ended up in being sex oriented got caught in a sex cobweb because there was no proper direction on where the relationship was going. I beg you to not get yourself in a relationship when you are not ready to marry.

Prayer points

- Lord Jesus, I terminate any contract that has landed me in a terrible relationship in the name of Jesus

- Lord, give me the courage to break a relationship that is leading nowhere in the name of Jesus

- My time shall not be wasted in a useless relationship the name of Jesus

- Evil powers seeking to take me through heartbreaks, you will not succeed in the name of Jesus

- I am not a candidate of wasted emotions in the name of Jesus

CHAPTER FOURTEEN

PREPARING FOR A RELATIONSHIP

Somebody said, "Failure to prepare is preparing to fail." This is true regarding relationships.

Relationships are a very sensitive part of our hearts and since hearts are fragile, one should not thoughtlessly jump into a relationship. Because relationships involve ones emotions, they are to be handled with care because if not, they have potential to break you down.

You should prepare for a relationship before you can enter into it. You must be aware of what is involved in it.

Below are eight ways you can prepare for a relationship:

1. Desire a relationship

You must have a genuine desire for a relationship. If you don't desire a relationship, you are not ready to get into one. Desire is a sign that there is a motivation for you to get in a relationship.

2. Develop a positive attitude about relationships

If you don't have a healthy positive attitude about relationships, you are not ready for one. No normal person will want to involve himself or herself in a relationship with a person that has a negative attitude about relationships. Attitudes such as the notion that all men or ladies are the same should be dealt with before you engage yourself in a relationship. It is not true that all people are the same. It is a lie. That is a blanket statement. The man who wants to date you may not be like that crook who cheated on you.

3. Discern a relationship when its coming

Unusual compliments from someone, constant communication, unusual kindness, special treatments, etc. are all points for discerning a relationship. You must be able to tell when someone is interested in you or not. They can pretend to be your prayer partner but soon the emotions will erupt like a volcano and you will know why you were being treated that way but you have to discern their moves. Don't chase away someone whom you may be happy to date by your insensitive attitude. For

God's sake he/she has never bought you a Christmas card before, why now?

4. *Destroy past failures regarding relationships*

Most people have stories to tell from their love life journeys. Many of these stories have a happy beginning but a sad ending. It is the sad ending in some love journeys that cause people to develop a suspicious and unhealthy attitude about relationships. You should clear all the failures of your past before you can enter into a new relationship. In short, start your love life on a whole new page.

5. *Declare your interest in a relationship*

You must be seen to be interested in being in a relationship but don't show signs of desperation. You should never be heard by potential partners making funny of being in a relationship, you will chase them away. Openly, share your interest in being loved and loving someone. This approach will attract likeminded people to you.

6. Declare your readiness for a relationship

If you are serious about getting into a relationship, let not people hear you pretentiously despise relationships. Declare your readiness for a relationship. For example tell the people interested to know when you wish to get married.

7. Determine readiness for a relationship

You must be able to gage your readiness for a relationship. Look at whatever plans you have made and the goals you have set for yourself to determine whether you are ready to commit yourself to someone or not. If you are not ready for marriage and will not be ready any time soon, I advise that you keep away from involving yourself in a relationship because you will one day live to regret the time you spent trying to take a relationship to nowhere. Marriage should be the absolute direction to take for any relationship.

8. Divine guidance is to be sort before you get in a relationship

Seek divine guidance before you commit yourself to anybody. Pray about it. if you are already head over hill about the whole thing try your best to hung on a little longer and ask other Christian believers to pray with you over the matter before you can commit.

Prayer points

- Lord, help me to know when am ready for a relationship in the name of Jesus
- Lord, help me to know when I am not ready for a relationship in the name of Jesus
- I shall not waste my time pursuing a relationship heading nowhere in the name of Jesus
- Lord, when I am ready for a relationship I pray that you will help me not to repel the partner you send my way in the name of Jesus
- Lord, give me the right attitude that will attract right people into my life in the name of Jesus

Amen

CHAPTER FIFTEEN

SEVEN RELATIONSHIP KILLERS

A relationship can start all good with love and understand but along the way, two people can start to take advantage of each other; taking each other for granted and thus end up bringing conflict in a relationship that if not checked can lead to a terrible end of a relationship that started on a good note. Below are seven relationship killers.

1. *Criticism*

Criticism dampens the morale and zest of the person being criticized. In a relationship, you will want your partner to be an encouragement to you and not your critic. Of course there is what is called positive criticism but I would rather call it advice and not criticism. The word criticism carries a natural connotation of negativity and it can really bring tension in a relationship and even lead to its failure. Watch your critical attitude. It could be the reason why your partner prefers to be around other people than you.

2. Lying

Lying is a terrible vice in relationships. It is so painful to be lied to by someone you love. You always want your partner to say the truth no matter how hard it is. Truth heals but lying hurts and worsens the wound. Avoid the so called white lies. They are not as white as they often seem they are usually pure black and the damage they will cause to your relationship may be so severe and beyond repair. Learn to tell the truth. E.g. don't say you are driving when you are actually lying in bed chewing bubble gum!

3. Failure to forgive

There is no one that is perfect. Every person has his or her own flows. You should be ready to forgive your partner when they wrong you. Un-forgiveness kills relationships. Learn to forgive and forget. Forgetting does not mean you cannot completely remember what your partner deed but you don't use it to get at them.

Forgiveness is a powerful quality of being. Many relationships that we have celebrated have had their strength drawn from this awesome quality of forgiveness. It is not that the two love bird would never fly away from each other but it is because just when one of them was about to fly away, the other was quick to acknowledge its faults by saying sorry and the offended bird decided to stay on just that once.

Before you can quit a relationship because your partner has offended you, you need you take stock of the many things they have done, both good and bad and you will actually realize they have done more good than bad things. Count the good and tolerate the bad.

4. Busyness

If you are so busy for your relationship, be assured that your relationship is going downhill to failure. You must make time for your partner no matter what and when your partner makes time for you, be grateful. Nowadays people are so careful on how they use their time so when someone makes time for you, it's not a right. It is a privilege that someone else has offered you because they are responsible so do not take it for granted.

5. Selfishness

Learn to share in your relationship. Let me in particular address ladies on this point. Dear ladies, get rid of the mind-set that you are just recipients. You must develop an attitude of giving to you partner.

Selfishness will kill your relationship. It is a vice that you must not ignore. Fight it with gestures of generosity by doing something special for your partner.

6. Pride

Watch out for pride. Don't be proud. Learn to acknowledge your mistakes and admit ignorance on what you don't know. Pride will destroy harmony in your relationship. In fact, the bible says, pride comes before the fall.

Oh! For heaven's sake you don't know it all so be humble to respect your partner's views and give them a benefit of doubt that they could be right and you could be wrong.

7. Sin

If you are living in sin in your relationship, you are inviting trouble and untold sorrows on your relationship. Sin, especially sexual is a deadly poison that will in no time accumulate in the life line of your relationship and will chock it until it dies.

Prayer points

- I refuse to be a critic in my relationship in the name of Jesus
- I refuse to be a liar in my relationship in the name of Jesus
- Lord God, give me the grace to forgive my partner in the name of Jesus
- I refuse to assassinate my relationship by being unreasonably busy for my partner in the name of Jesus
- I refuse to be selfish and self centered in this relationship in the name of Jesus

- I bind and reject the spirit of pride in my heart that is working against my relationship in then name of Jesus

- Every power of sin working against my relationship I reject your influence and effect on my life and relationship in the name of Jesus

- My relationship shall not die in the name of Jesus. Amen

In conclusion, I hope the thoughts in this book have been helpful as various issues concerning relationships have been addressed. I do wish you a happy love life and God bless you. Take time to pray the following prayers for your love life in the name of Jesus and I declare that God will answer your prayers. Amen.

1. Father in heaven, thank you for your word says it is not good for me to be alone in the name of Jesus

2. Father in heaven thank you for the partner you have or yet to send my way in the name of Jesus

3. Father in heaven, I refuse to get married to a anybody who will come to quench the fire of the holy ghost in my life in the name of Jesus

4. My heart, reject any wrong person showing interest in me in the name of Jesus

5. Every power of the devil seeking to frustrate my destiny by bringing a godless person to marry me, that power shall not succeed in the name of Jesus

6. My God sent partner, appear and locate me without any further delays in the name of Jesus

7. I call forth my grand wedding in the name of Jesus

8. (for sister) I shall not fall pregnant outside the wedlock in the name of Jesus. The spirit of shall not locate me in the name of Jesus

9. (for brothers) I shall not make pregnant any woman who is not my wife in the name of Jesus. The spirit of shame shall not locate me in the name of Jesus

10. I receive the grace of sexual purity in the name of Jesus

11. I shall not be rejected by my God sent partner in the name of Jesus

12. I shall not be dumped by my God sent partner in the name of Jesus

13. Anyone desiring to snatch my God sent partner, you are a liar, you will not succeed in the name of Jesus

14. I refuse to get married to a none believer in the name of Jesus

15. Time waster shall not locate me in the name of Jesus

16. I shall not attract a married person to date me in the name of Jesus

17. Every evil mask hiding my beauty/handsomeness, fall off my face in the name of Jesus

18. Every power of wickedness, obstructing the good virtues that God has put in me from my God sent man, you evil power, I break your hold on me in the name of Jesus

19. I wear spiritual perfume to attract my God sent partner in the name of Jesus

20. My relationship shall successfully lead to a happy marriage in the name of Jesus

Recommended readings

- Boy meets girl by Joshua Harris

- Before you do by Td Jakes

- Marriage covenant by Derik Prince

- Keeping your covenant published by Family Life.

- Effective marriage by Nancy Van Pelt

- 10 secrets of a great marriage by Lilo and Gerard Leeds

www.ingramcontent.com/pod-product-compliance
Lightning Source LLC
Chambersburg PA
CBHW060806050426
42449CB00008B/1555